Choose a topic and start to practise writing. Each booklet has a theme to help you start to write…stories, reports, articles, letters and many more. Start collecting them now.

Guinea Pig creative writing booklets also provide extra practice for children who have completed:

- Creative Story Writing ISBN: 9780955831508
- Persuasive Writing & Argument ISBN: 9780955831515
- Information Writing ISBN: 9780955831522

They are for:

* children who are working at Key Stage 2 of the National Curriculum, levels 3-5 (in Years 5 and 6 of primary school),
* children who are working at Key Stage 3, levels 3-5 (Years 7 and 8 of Secondary School).

They provide practice for all 9-13 year olds, especially children taking 11+ examinations.



Written by Sally A Jones and Amanda C Jones

Published by GUINEA PIG EDUCATION

2 Cobs Way,
New Haw,
Addlestone,
Surrey,
KT15 3AF.

www.guineapigeducation.co.uk

# Let's **learn** to *write* <u>non-fiction</u>.

When you *write non-fiction*, <u>**you may write**</u>:

- a newspaper report

- an information leaflet

- instructions

- a diary entry.

**<u>You must decide</u>**:

1. Who will be my target audience?

2. Who will read this writing?

3. What is the purpose of my writing?

**The form might be:** an information leaflet

**The audience might be:** older primary school children (9-11 years)

**The purpose might be:** to inform them about some facts

# **Plan** your non-fiction writing:

<table>
<tr><td>

**PARAGRAPH 1**

- Introduce the reader to your topic.

- Give some facts about your chosen subject.

</td><td>

</td></tr>
<tr><td>

**PARAGRAPH 2, 3, 4...**

- Write down the points you want to make in chronological order.

- Back them up with evidence.

</td><td>

**Remember:**

- Use connectives or conjunctions:

  - *and or but (to join compound sentences)*
  - *or, so, if, when, while, after, before, because, unless, until, whereas, although (to join complex sentences)*
  - *use pronouns - who, which, whose, what, that*
  - *to link ideas use - firstly, later, therefore, on the other hand, at that moment, by this time, next, soon...*

- Use a range of sentences – simple, compound and complex sentences

</td></tr>
<tr><td>

**Conclusion**

- Draw all your ideas together in a conclusion.

</td><td>

- Make personal comments

</td></tr>
</table>

You have purchased a multi purpose school holdall. What do you think about it? Write about it for your school magazine.

## I highly recommend it:

This amazing bag changes to suit your requirements. You can strap it to your back as you walk to school; you can carry it from class to class; or you can push it along on its wheels. It is essential for school children who have to walk long distances with heavy books. It is so durable, it can be taken into space.

If you have an aching back every single night, the new multi purpose school holdall is for you. It is made of a revolutionary new material which feels as light as a feather. When you fill it up with your schoolbooks, it will not feel heavy at all. You will no longer feel as if you are lugging round a heavy bag. In fact, you will not even feel tired at the end of a long day at school.

What is more, the bag looks very trendy. It is the bag for all aspiring space men. It comes in a choice of bright fashionable colours; in vibrant purple, turquoise and pink. The design is stylish and really up to date. This bag is definitely something that will catch on, which young people will want to have as a fashion accessory. You will look really cool as you walk round school with it.

In addition to this, the bag is very functional. It is more roomy than any other bag, with plenty of room for your bulging pencil case, several large books and that plastic container that contains your lunch. There are hidden pockets concealed in the lining, where you can store your mobile phone or keys and access them quickly. Imagine this! It will enable you to be completely organised from now on.

Some people say that the bag is just a fashion gimmick; it is not made to last. They say it will start to look tatty after a few journeys home in pouring rain. I have had my bag for over a month and I can tell you that it is made of high quality material, being 100% waterproof. I've never had a bag that protected all my school things, so there's not one soggy page. If it gets dirty, you can just wipe it with a soft, damp cloth and the stains will disappear like magic.

Lastly, this bag offers the best value for money. It is cheap, compared to others in the shops, so that most pupils could afford one. It would also make a good present which is very reasonably priced. This bag is an innovation. It has changed the way I think about school. I definitely believe everyone should get one because they're worth every penny.

**I would not recommend it:**

Have you ever seen anything as ridiculous as the new Space Age school holdall. It is just a fashion gimmick that will be here today and gone tomorrow. The children of the future will wonder what we were doing, wheeling these hideous bags around on wheels.

You say that they fold up into a small bag that can be hung up, but as far as I can see, they are taking up lots of room in the cloakroom, parked like cars all over the place.

Besides this, they claim to be made of lightweight material, but they are as heavy as any normal bag when filled with schoolbooks. After carrying one around for two days, I had rubbed up a huge red blister on my shoulder, which was painful and sore.

In addition to this, if it was taken up to space it would disintegrate because the quality is poor and it is badly made. I had to return my first bag to the shop and get a replacement. After using it twice, the stitching on the seam started to come undone and it split open letting rainwater seep in which made my homework diary soggy.

The colours are shocking too. They are so bright; they are hideous and make your eyes sting. They are not even very fashionable because they don't have any of the latest logos. There is little room inside; everything is cramped up in a small space and you have to search frantically to find anything at all.

Finally, the price is horrendous. They cost twice as much as other similar bags, but this product is not as good. What is wrong with having a normal rucksack? You know, a traditional one, coloured black or blue, the kind people have always carried round, that will coordinate with your school uniform so you are a good representative of the school, not looking as if you are preparing for a camping holiday. Do not be tempted to get one because you will be wasting your money.

Now it is your turn to review a bag you have used. Write an article for your school magazine. Read the next two pages.

A new bag called the 'Space Age Holdall' has been invented, which will solve the problem of having to carry around heavy books all day. It has been invented by an engineering student, who spent many years carrying round a heavy bag of books. He designed it to help kids like yourself. Is it worth getting one?

Use the following questions to help you write the rest of the magazine article. Firstly, decide whether you are for or against the bag.

- What is the design like…?
- …and how does it work?

- What material is it made of?
- Is it heavy?

- What is it like to carry round?

- Is it trendy?
- Describe the colours, the style and the logos.
- Is it a good fashion accessory?

- Will it be out of date soon?

- How functional is it?
- Is there plenty of room?
- Are there extra pockets?
- What could you put in it?

- How can you store it when you are not using it?
- Are there compartments for your mobile phone?
  and for your lunch box?
- Will it last for a long time? (Is it durable?)

- Is it good quality?
- Is it well made?
- Is it waterproof?
- Will it keep everything dry?

- What is your opinion of the bag?
- Would you recommend it to your friends?
- Is it expensive to buy? Is it cheap?
- Does it offer good value for money?
- Does it have some shortcomings? In your opinion are there some things wrong with it?

⊙ Write a conclusion…

For example:

You can see it's definitely worth purchasing one of these bags. You will have an up date, designer bag, which is extremely practical as well. It is cheap to buy, but still made to last. It is definitely worth buying one of these bags

Here are extracts from reviews written by children with some points for and against the new bag.

During the last month I have used the 'Space Age Holdall' to carry my school books and equipment. The new bag looks very stylish. The colour and design are very fashionable. I like the fact that it is made from waterproof material so that my books remain dry even on extremely wet days. Last Wednesday, I got soaked returning from school, but all my possessions remained in perfect condition, safely stored in my bag.

At the same time, I found the bag very roomy so there was enough space to store my bulgy pencil case, my heavy school books, reading folder, the large plastic container and flask that contain my lunch and drink. As there are several outside pockets, I could put my flask and dinner in one so there was no danger of it spilling out.

However, I did find the bag very heavy to carry around on my back all day. I had to rub some cream on my shoulder, as it was so sore. Then I noticed that one of the straps was showing signs of coming unstitched. My mum tried to sew it, but the weight of my school project books tore the seam open again.

I think the bag needs to be made of much stronger material. It needs to be made in a darker coloured fabric so it doesn't show dirty marks. I would recommend you get one of these bags.

The new bag is not very stylish. I thought the colour and design was rather old fashioned and more suitable to take on a camping holiday. The material is also not completely waterproof. Last Wednesday, it was pouring with rain all day. I discovered, on returning home from school, that my homework folder was quite damp and the water had soaked in through the opening, which is only fastened by a strap.

I did not find the bag very roomy. There were lots of small pockets, but they were too small to fit anything in. For example, my pencil case was too long. The actual bag did not have enough space to fit all my books, my homework folder or my lunch container. I ended up carrying my plastic lunch box in my hand.

However, I did find the bag was light to carry round on my back. It was strong enough to hold heavy books without tearing the seam. I think it would last several years.

In my opinion, the company should redesign this bag with young people in mind. It should be much more fashionable in a bright colour with a logo on it. To hold more books, it needs to be designed so that it is wider with separate compartments. It could also have a zip fastening to keep everything safe and dry in bad weather. I don't recommend the bag.

Now write the magazine article you planned.

# The *'***SPACE AGE***'* Bag...
## ...*is <u>not</u> just a BAG!*

The Space Age bag takes you far away into outer space. Describe your trip in the space rocket. What would space flight be like? How would you use the bag? Is it multi functional?

It teaches you everything you need to know about space:

**Did you know you grow more than 2 inches taller when you are in space!**

**Did you know astronauts sleep in sleeping bags attached to the wall!**

The space bag contains a computer that can teach you everything about space.

*Use the internet or an encyclopedia to answer the following questions:*

- How many planets are there in the solar system?

.................................................................................................................

- Can you name them?

.................................................................................................................

- Which planet is known as the red planet?

.................................................................................................................

- What is the closest planet to the sun?

.................................................................................................................

- Does the sun orbit the earth?

.................................................................................................................

- Is the sun a planet or a star?

.................................................................................................................

- Who was the first man on the moon?

.................................................................................................................

- Which was the first living creature to be launched into space?

.................................................................................................................

- Can human beings breathe normally in space, as they can on earth?

.................................................................................................................

- What is the name of NASA's famous space telescope?

.................................................................................................................

- What is the name of the force holding us on earth?

.................................................................................................................

- How long does it take to travel from earth to the moon?

.................................................................................................................

- Which is the only planet in the solar system, where scientists have found evidence of water having existed and which could hence have sustained life in the past?

.................................................................................................................

**Imagine there has been advances in space travel and you can travel through light years to distant universes very quickly.** Write about your flight into outer space. Use the notes below to help you. You can write it in the form of a narrative (story) or as a diary.

### Write what the take off is like

Launch space rocket

Lay flat on back

Strapped in seat

Astronaut suit on

Hear the great build up of power in the engine – 'whoosh'

Pulled back into your seat as space rocket launches into sky

Zoom – up, up, up deep into outer space

### Write what it is like travelling in outer space

See blackness

See earth shrinking

Earth is a tiny ball in the distance

Travelling thousands of miles in minutes

Travelling fifty light years to a new universe in a different solar system

Everything weightless

Floating in space

How did your space age bag help you?

Does it contain all of your provisions for living in space – an i pod, C.D.s, earth food and earth water? How does it store all of these provisions? How can it be used? Can it double up as a seat – a pillow- a table – any other ideas?

### Write about visiting another planet

What planet are you orbiting?

Do the aliens know you're there?

Are you going to send a shuttle down?

What provisions do you put into your space age bag? Would you take gifts for the aliens from earth? Which gifts would you choose? Would you take photographs of earth? What would the photographs be of? Would you take weapons to protect yourself in case the aliens are dangerous – maybe a space gun that makes the aliens freeze?

Now write the story or diary entry you planned.

Write about some more school products you
have used.  You can use your imagination.

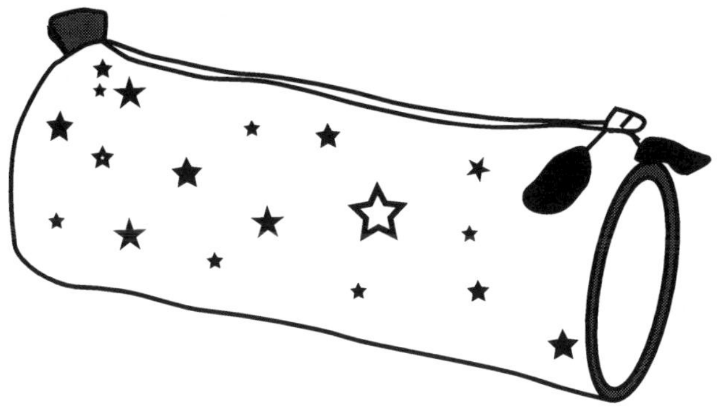

I bought a new Space
Age pencil case that:

- cleans rubbers
- sharpens pencils
- refills pens with ink.

At the supermarket my mum got me a new super Space Age lunch box that keeps food hot or cold.

For my birthday, I had a new computer notebook. You speak your homework tasks into it and it writes your homework for you.

Write your answers in the boxes.

# APEX

### The NEW Space Nutrition Tablets

APEX delicious meals are now available in tablet form. All you have to do is dissolve a tablet in space water and your meal is ready!
There are thirty delicious flavours to choose from: lasagne, pizza, apple crumble or chocolate ice cream, for example. APEX is the cheapest and most nutritious space food on the market.

..................................................
..................................................
..................................................
..................................................
..................................................
..................................................
..................................................
..................................................
..................................................
..................................................
..................................................
..................................................

# NASA
## SPACE SUITS

**NASA is now selling AMAZING SPACE SUITS at 50% off RRP.**

The suits come with a UV protective helmet, jet pack and cool air tank. NASA suits are designed to protect you when you are in space. What's more they are incredibly comfortable.

Hurry! Stock is limited.

**Design a pair of super 'Space Age' trainers 'CHEATERS'. Write about them for your school magazine.**

The trainers are the latest design, including:

- Cool colours
- Design logo on instep

The trainers are made of the best materials:

- The trainers have a rubber sole that is so springy.
- It makes you want to do exercise…to run and jump higher and to pedal longer.

They are functional and can be worn to compete in all sports, in competitions and for going out on the weekend.

You'll be in inter school sports because you'll run as fast as a cheater.

You will never slip over again because the soles have magnets in them, which make you stick to the ground.

They are great value for money:

- Cheaters are available in supermarkets and high street stores.
- They are a competitive price.
- They are durable and will last you a long time.

<u>Evaluation</u>

Write about famous people who wear these trainers?

*'Cheaters' are worn by ….. famous footballers and celebrities.*

What do they say?

*"These trainers are the best around. I could not train without them…"*

What do you think of the trainer? What did you find that was not so good about them?

Make up some designer trainers.  Write about them for your school magazine.

**Let's plan a story.**

| | |
|---|---|
| **Introduction**<br><br>Introduce:<br><br>    • Characters<br>    • Setting<br>    • Plot | Boy buys a Space Age Bag.<br><br>Takes it home and puts school books in it. |
| **Middle**<br><br>• Develop the plot. Action is triggered by a conflict or complication that needs to be solved.<br>• Build up tension | Takes it to school.<br><br>Bullies steal it. |
| **Ending or Conclusion**<br><br>• Problem solved<br>• Wind story up | Head teacher finds out who stole it.<br><br>Boys caught and punished. |

# The Space Age Bag

Charles Frederick Augustus was a clever boy, who always got top grades. His ambition was to be an engineer, so he knew he had to work hard. That's why he always did his homework on time. In fact, he spent two hours every night working at his desk. He didn't watch T.V. and he didn't play on his computer, unless he was completely satisfied he'd got all the facts down, answered every question and done his best effort. There was only one problem. Charles Frederick had so many books he needed for all his subjects. He lugged them around in his worn out old bag that he'd had for three years. They were so heavy. By the time he arrived home, after a tiring school day, he slumped down on his bed. Exhausted!

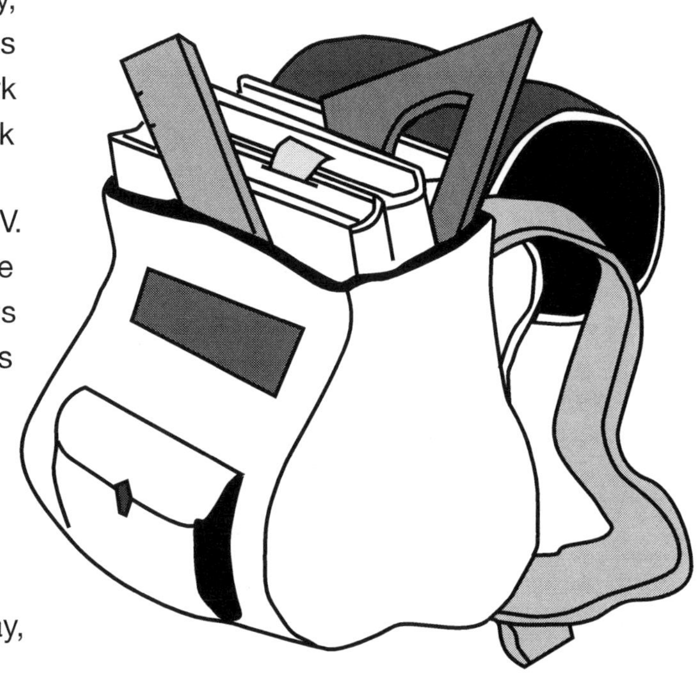

At the start of the new term, he asked his mum, "Can I have a new school bag?"
"Of course," she said, "I'll get one from the catalogue."
"No. I mean a real bag, a designer one. I want a Space Age bag. You see them advertised on T.V. If you get one, it will give you special powers and fill your head with space facts. I'll be a genius at school mum. Please, please."
"I'm not sure. They're quite expensive."
"They'll last ages, because they're really strong. It says so on T.V. They have loads of room in them, lots of separate compartments and you can wheel them around. It'll save you money in the long run. You won't have to buy cream for my sore shoulder," where my old bag rubs up a blister. Mum reluctantly agreed that she would look into it. She always spoiled Charles Frederick because he was an only child and so she gave him most things he needed.

On Saturday they went to the High Street to the Space Age designer store. It sold high quality items. They looked at all the new Space Age bags that were for sale. An assistant came over and demonstrated one.
"Look," he said, "it's easy to wheel with these rotating wheels and then just shake it back up to a normal bag. It folds down really small for storage." Charles Frederick chose a purple one. The assistant packed it in a bag, with the shiny logo printed on it. Amazing! How proud he felt. He would be the envy of his class mates. On arriving home, he packed his bag ready for Monday morning.

* * * * * * * * * * * * * * * * * * * *

Piers and Oliver looked at each other across the table.
"Have you seen Charles's new bag?" whispered Piers. "It's new. It's one of those on T.V. Trust him to have one that's better than the rest of us," he smirked.
"I think we should teach him a lesson. When it's home time, I'll get him into conversation about the football match and you get the bag." This is what they did. They stole the bag. They took it out of school and on the way home, they chucked it over the hedge. They left it there.

Charles Frederick's mum sat in the car. She waited ages and ages. There was no one left in the playground. In the end, she got out of the car and went in to search for Charles. He was searching the cloakroom with his teacher. His new designer Space Age bag had disappeared. They searched and searched, but it was nowhere to be seen. It had gone! Charles was devastated. His mum was furious. He sat with his head between his hands in the car, trying to work out his last movements. Had he been talking to Piers?

A smart lady, who lived in a residential street close to the school, appeared at the gate. The children watched her. She strolled briskly towards the head teacher's office. She had a stern look on her face. She had something to complain about. "It's like this," she said to Mr Watson, "I was having tea outside in my garden, enjoying the sun, when a huge bag came hurtling over my fence.  I thought it was going to hit me but it missed me and fell in the pond and sunk. I can't get it because it's right in the middle in deep water."
"Do you know who did this?" replied the head teacher with a serious expression on his face.
"I peered round the fence and caught sight of two boys dressed in the uniform of this school," answered the smart lady.

Mr Watson called an emergency assembly. He took the matter really seriously. He said a bag has been thrown into a neighbour's garden. Some children from this school have behaved badly. They've let the school down. He said that he intended to find out who those children were. He asked anyone to come forward if they knew who did it. Otherwise he would have a detention for the whole school. Charles Frederick's ears pricked up. He had lost a bag, but he certainly hadn't thrown it over the hedge of Mrs Gilmore's garden. It had been stolen. His mind worked overtime as he considered the evidence... He concluded that the last person he had spoken to had been Piers. He couldn't have taken it, could he? What about his friend Oliver? Charles looked over at them. At that moment, they exchanged glances and  . sniggered at each other. That afternoon, Charles went to see the head teacher and told him what he suspected.

Mr Watson took the whole situation very seriously. He insisted on speaking to the two boys immediately. They looked white, pale and silent. They soon caved in.
"He suggested it, Sir," whimpered Oliver sheepishly.
"No I didn't. It was you."
"You're admitting to this action. You will miss break time for three weeks. You will be given jobs around the school, tidying up litter. You will both provide money to buy Charles a new bag. This is what happened, and with the money, Charles mum bought him a deluxe version of the Space Age bag. Soon, the whole class were wheeling their new bags along, except for Piers and Oliver, who kept their old ones.

Now, try writing this story in 3 paragraphs - with a beginning, a middle and an ending.

● The longer story has several characters: Charles, Mum, Piers, Oliver, head teacher, the neighbour Mrs Gilmore. Write one or two sentences about each one and how they react to other people.

The story moves its setting. Write about: Charles home, the shop, the school, the cloakroom Describe each setting in one or two sentences.

The plot is developed in each paragraph. Write a sentence to say what happens in each paragraph.

The story is in ............ person – so it is told by a narrator.

It is in ............ tense.

Charlotte Louise gets a new pair of 'super trainers' – Space Age trainers, but somehow they get swapped over during a P.E. lesson. Now it is your turn to tell Louise's story.

## Make a plan:

| | |
|---|---|
| **<u>Introduction</u>**<br><br>Introduce:<br><br>    • Characters<br>    • Setting<br>    • Plot | |
| **<u>Middle</u>**<br><br>• Develop the plot. Action is triggered off by a conflict or complication that needs to be solved.<br>• Build up tension | |
| **<u>Ending or Conclusion</u>**<br><br>• Problem solved<br>• Wind story up | |

Now write the story you planned.

Made in the USA
Monee, IL
07 July 2026

56644842R00015